THE
END
OF
ACTING
TECHNIQUE

THE BOOKS BY LARRY SILVERBERG

"Larry Silverberg's new book *The End of Acting Technique* is a love letter to the art and craft of acting. Silverberg masterfully peels away layer after layer of intellectual acting class subterfuge to lay bare the path to honesty in performance. This book is a gift to actors of all levels as well as acting teachers who seek to reexamine what actor training in America is, can and should be about; it is an invitation to begin the real work of an actor, the deep exploration of what it means to be authentic in performance, and in life."

Anjalee Deshpande Hutchinson
Associate Professor of Theatre & Dance; Department Chair.
Bucknell University

"Larry Silverberg's *The End of Acting Technique* explores an approach that unleashes the actor into the free, spontaneous and intuitive space required for the intimacy of a film performance.

This book will inspire all actors to practice the art of acting at the highest possible level. Students of the art of acting as well as seasoned professionals will find this book indispensable. I highly recommend it."

Professor Timothy Hagan
Film Acting Teacher & Director/Founder The OC Film
School
Olympic College, Bremerton, Washington

"Adding to his impressive collection of books on acting, Larry Silverberg's latest provides a clear, coherent and inspiring methodology, leading to the thrill of authentic discovery.

Larry gives us an inspiring set of principles that free that actor from the myriad of the weighty intellectual approaches of the past. This book is a must for all artistic truth seekers. It's more than a guidebook for acting. It's a guidebook for living an authentic life."

Gregory Ramos
Chair, Professor and Resident Director
University of Vermont

"Larry's book demystifies the acting process. Profoundly simple truths, this book is a touchstone for actors of all levels."

Jerry Cohagan, Theatre director/professor-Olivet
Nazarene University

"As Acting teachers, we should be constantly searching for guidance to help our students become their best selves. In *The End of Acting Technique*, Mr. Silverberg has given us a clear, concise roadmap to do just that.

With succinct language and online exercises, he reminds us to look past the "gobbledygook" and to recapture what brought us to the theatre in the first place; the true and alive humanness of relationship, the utter simplicity of being and the pure joy of expression.

You want to "unclog" yourself as an actor and reclaim the freedom to be? Then read this book right now, right now, right now!!!"

Angela Dickson, actor/instructor
Alabama Shakespeare Festival

"Larry has written the most specific and accurate book I have ever read on acting, it is the book I wish I could have found when I started in the profession. He pinpoints all of the essential needs of our acting job. Follow Larry step by step and you'll feel more and more confident, more and more alive, more authentic, and quickly you'll find the light of yours that you will never want to lose again.

You feel lost in your acting? This book is meant for you.

You're getting bored in your acting? This book is meant for you.

You want to boost your career ? This book is meant for you.

Thanks Larry for this amazing book. I'll recommend it to all actors, wherever they are in their career."

Catherine Zavlav
French Film and Television Actress & Acting Coach

"*The End of Acting Technique* by Larry Silverberg, encompasses Larry's experience of decades of dedication to the craft of acting, summarized with great clarity and effectiveness, offering a simple way to reach the heart of the work. Silverberg renounces all technicalities, he illuminates with precision and essentiality the fundamental passages for an authentic, living acting as he demystifies all useless or misleading acting concepts.

With generosity and mastery, distilled in years of searching for truth and "life itself" in the theater, the book takes us to the space where the actor accesses his "creative zone", where the work of each artist is special, rare, unique.

This book is a precious tool for every actor fully committed to his art, and for teachers and directors who wish to accompany actors in the creative process, providing them with the keys to transformation.

With Larry's organic and human approach to the craft, you will be led to being in the flow, being deeply available, attentive and sensitive. You will learn that acting is a more honest relationship with yourself and with others: it is a deeper access to your life, a powerful and joyful way to express your true self. This book reminds us and shows us how to do it.

Larry has given us a necessary text, written with the precision that only the great ones possess."

Irina Casali, Actress, Director, Teacher
Acting Languages Academy, Milan

"Do yourself a favor and open this book. What happens then is not really about reading, what happens is you "experience" the book. As the true master he is, Larry Silverberg not only gives you essential keys on acting, simple and pragmatic, but he creates a kind of intimate dialog with you and a space that allows you to become a "top 5% actor."

Whatever your relation to acting is, as you turn the pages, two things are growing in you: a huge relief, and a striving force that urges you to go on the stage."

Ludovic Girard
Actor/Teacher, France

"This book is a must read for those new to acting as well as for those who are experienced. Larry has a unique way of communicating and teaching the art of acting - in a simple, direct, meaningful and respectful way, spiced with humor and a love for the craft. When you read it, you want to start working.

Never has acting been communicated so clearly. You will never accept artificial moments or direction again. When reading this book, you will know that acting is about being alive - no more, no less."

Frank Lofqvist
Renowned acting facilitator and leadership trainer, Denmark

"I teach acting to 9th -12th grade theatre students who are already, at their young age, mired in bad habits, social anxieties and complex self-images. Getting them to give in to process over product, work in the "right now" is a challenge. Larry's insights, revealed in the pages of this book, will encourage young actors to work from a place of instinct, intuition and unfettered understanding of their own human natures.

I use Larry's books, exercises and analogies to great effect with my students and watch them live, respond and act in meaningful, personal ways. Larry puts things in such simple straight-forward ways, demystifying and purifying the alchemy of acting."

Scott Keys,
Booker Visual and Performing Arts High School
Sarasota, FL

"*The End of Acting Technique* is another pedagogical gem by master teacher, Larry Silverberg!

Silverberg takes the ambiguity out of the acting process by presenting us with his succinct, well-defined approach. Most importantly, he provides us with proven tools which will strengthen our skills and help us become innovative artists.

I feel such gratitude towards Larry Silverberg. Even after many years of teaching and training he has helped me to become a better teacher, performer, writer and person. When my students ask me who they should study with after they graduate, I direct them to Larry! "

Lesley-Ann Timlick,
Professor/artist, author and researcher
with a focus on training diverse actors
Florida International University, Miami

"There is a lifetime's worth of wisdom distilled into *The End of Acting Technique* and it's the only book about acting you'll ever need. This is a master class from a master teacher. I love it!!"

Anne Swedberg, Theatre Professor
University of Tennessee at Chattanooga

"Larry Silverberg cares deeply about actors and acting and his insights make a vital contribution to the craft. In *The End of Acting Technique*, he has distilled his many years of teaching experience into a gem of a book destined to be on every actors' required reading list.

Beautifully refined and crafted, Larry's writing is deeply inspirational. As an acting teacher, this book makes me even more excited to work with acting students. As an actor, it inspires me to reconsider my practice and ignites my longing to dive deeper into the work. Larry always finds a way to sharpen and refine the craft. A must read."

Valerie Campbell, Associate Professor
School of Creative and Performing Arts - Drama
University of Calgary

"*The End of Acting Technique* is overwhelming in its pure and direct honesty of what acting should be. It is an incredible guideline for both how to become a great actor and what it really means to be human. Larry writes as he teaches, in the most inspiring way you can imagine."

Lou Binder, Director, Munich Film Academy
Munich, Germany

"Larry Silverberg crushes it in *The End of Acting Technique*. It is one of the most effective books about acting that I have read. Silverberg wrote it with his heart and shares with passion and love all the knowledge he has.

The evolution of true acting is found in this revolutionary book. It is a guide for actors to live truthfully every time they perform. It offers the path for success to any committed actor. It teaches what good, real and honest acting really is.

The End of Acting Technique injected life into me as an acting instructor. I'm more equipped to support students in their journey; to help them be ready and prepared to bring life on camera or on stage. Thank you, Larry, for pointing the way!"

Yvia Neves
Acting Teacher, Chicago

"*The End of Acting Technique* is the essence, it is distilled knowledge. It's like perfume. It gets straight to your heart. The message is simple, crystal clear and friendly. It gave me great joy and motivation. I have found in Larry's words a new strength to work and create with great freedom because he gives us the most powerful tools for the modern actor. Thank you Larry for your wonderful contribution to the acting community worldwide."

Laura Moise
TAS Acting Studio, Valencia, Spain

"*The End of Acting Technique*, by Larry Silverberg turns intellectual, heady approaches to acting upside down. And like all things profound, there's great depth in the simplicity and clarity of Larry's approach. It is at once practical and inspiring."

Connie de Veer, Professor
Director of Graduate Studies for the M.F.A.
School of Theatre and Dance, Illinois State University

"WOW," just "WOW"!!!! No one speaks to our heart and challenges the slick emptiness of theatre today like world renowned acting teacher and author, Larry Silverberg. No holds barred.

At long last, his quintessential book, *The End of Acting Technique*, demystifies and simplifies our profession like no other, cutting through all the intellectual bullshit, without denouncing it, in a way that only Larry can do. In his simple way, he challenges and inspires each of us, regardless of where we are in life to rise up into our full humanity and personal greatness and, in so doing, changes the trajectory of our art; indeed, our lives."

Gaye Burgess
Award winning theater professor
University of North Dakota, Retired

"In *The End of Acting Technique* Larry Silverberg cuts through the jargon that plagues today's acting schools and confuse and confound their students. Larry takes the unnecessary "mystery" out of acting and succinctly gets to the heart of what actors must do to bring life to the stage or screen. Larry's approach is simple, but demands an actor's heart, soul, mind, strength; and a commitment to the craft."

Steven Pounders,
Professor, Department of Theatre Arts
Baylor University

"Larry Silverberg is a master teacher and the collected wisdom of his years of training both actors and acting teachers is contained in this book which boils the mystery of acting down to its very essence. All those who seek to act with deep personal meaning and relentless specificity will benefit from this practical and inspiring guide."

Robert Westenberg
Tony Nominated, Broadway Veteran
(*Into the Woods* and many others)
Professor of Theatre and Coordinator
BFA Musical Theatre Program
Missouri State University

"*The End of Acting Technique* is a true gift from master teacher Larry Silverberg. You hear his voice on each page; his desire, insight, and sense of humor. His teachings on "life itself" echo throughout. The book is indispensable for all students, teachers, and practitioners of acting. Thank you, Larry!"

Kato Buss, Ph.D., Chairperson, Associate Professor
Department of Theatre Arts
University of Central Oklahoma

"Master teacher Larry Silverberg's book *The End of Acting Technique* is revolutionary and awe inspiring. In plain English he details the path to creating "life itself" on stage and in film. For those brave enough to make a total commitment, this book that will guide them to results that are truly exceptional."

Mariah Reed
Professor of Theater
Broward College

THE
END
OF
ACTING
TECHNIQUE

LARRY
SILVERBERG

Smith & Kraus

A Smith and Kraus Book
PO Box 564 Hanover, NH 03755
editorial 603.643.6431 To Order 1.877.668.8680
www.smithandkraus.com

Manufactured in the United States of America

ISBN: 978-1-57525-943-7
Library of Congress Control Number: 2019947897

Typesetting and layout by Elizabeth E. Monteleone
Cover by Larry Silverberg

For information about custom editions, special sales, education
and corporate purchases, please contact Smith and Kraus
at editor@smithandkraus.com or 603.643.6431

For Jill

TABLE OF CONTENTS

Introduction.

The fact is, you can act.

To be absolutely clear...

You can act.

How do I know?

I know that you can act because...

You were born to act.

In fact...

You have already mastered the art. You just don't know it yet.

That's the point of this book.

I want you to know.

❖❖❖

1. I am interested in results, not theories.
2. I am going to take the mystery out of acting and show you how simple acting is.
3. The point of this book is to help you become what I call a "top 5% actor" right now.

❖❖❖

Over the years, my students have continually told me that they learned more in four weeks of my classes then they learned in many years of other actor training and in many years of working in the industry. I am going to share with you the ways of working I have discovered that get these results.

When you watch a play or a movie that is so real, so intimate, that it takes your breath away, the actors are in a space I call "the creative zone." This book will guide you there.

This is a book and an interactive website. At certain points in the book, I will invite you to join me online for a longer discussion, instruction and exercises.

The link is:

www.trueactinginstitute.com/learn

❖❖❖

PART ONE. SETTING THE STAGE

Chapter One.

The End of Acting Technique

a.

Am I saying that the time for acting technique is over?

No.

Am I saying that acting technique is no longer relevant?

No.

Am I saying that an actor does not need an acting technique?

Well...

All valid acting techniques are pointing towards one thing - helping you become a creative artist so that you are not an imitation of everything that has come before. Arriving at this place in your work is very special and very rare.

Do you need to study a particular technique to get there? Hold on to that question for now.

❖❖❖

b.

Every valid acting technique trains you in three major acting components.

That's it, just three.

Sound simple?

It is.

The good news is that you are already doing these three things. They are not foreign to you.

You can strengthen yourself in these three major acting components outside of a formal classroom.

❖❖❖

c.

Everyone can act. Everyone.

This means...

You can act.

I do not mean that you can "sort of" act...

I mean that you can be what I call, a "top 5% actor"

What about that frightening word, "talent?"

You do not need to worry about the word "talent" ever again.

You can throw that word away for good.

I have listened to many acting teachers complain that they, "wish they only had talented students."

I say. "There is something big lacking in those teachers, not in their students."

❖❖❖

d.

Major acting truth...

Acting is profoundly simple.

When I show this to you...

You will be profoundly encouraged.

❖❖❖

e.

I am writing this book to "demystify."

To demystify what?

To demystify what many acting classes have turned into a...

Confusing,

Inhuman,

Academic,

Bunch of gobbledygook.

Definition...

Gob·ble·dy·gook: unintelligible jargon; hard to understand; plain nonsense.

❖❖❖

f.

This book will totally transform everything you have thought about acting, it will be the breath of fresh air you have been longing for.

No mystery, no hype.

❖❖❖

Chapter Two.

Acting Technique: Does anybody really do one?

The question of this chapter: "Acting Technique: Does anybody really do one?"

The answer: "very few."

Consider this.

A.

All of the great teachers who created an approach to training actors, did it out of a life's devotion to the acting values they held dear. Stanislavsky, Sanford Meisner, Stella Adler, Lee Strasberg, Uta Hagan, etc., were all determined to find ways to do one thing - bring what I call "life itself" to the stage and in front of the camera.

MAJOR ACTING KEY:

Without "life itself," everything else will be without meaning or purpose. Meaning and purpose are the cornerstones of the craft.

If you decide on studying any particular technique of acting, I encourage you to consider this question and answer:

Question: If the master teachers spent a lifetime developing a way of working that helps actors arrive at "life itself," do you really think that anything other than your total devotion to any of these approaches will be of any use?

Answer: No, it won't.

Learning any of the great acting approaches will take your one hundred percent, relentless and total commitment. Of course, as in any aspect of life, once you make the commitment, you can expect that the challenges will come flooding in.

For example:

Many people commit to learning to play guitar. As soon as they begin to play, they discover very quickly, the tips of their fingers are in great pain as they try to press the strings down hard enough to play the notes. This is when most people will decide that guitar was not for them after all. "Hmm-mm..." they will say, "I was really meant to play the piano. I commit to learning piano." Very quickly, these people will discover that playing scales is very difficult. "Hmmmm..." they will say, "I was really meant to play the drums. I commit to learning the drums!" And on and on and on...

In learning the craft of acting, the challenges will be enormous and your commitment will be tested. You will question yourself, your abilities, your career choice, the teacher, your fellow students, the technique you are studying, the world around you, the universe.

This is where 95% of actors run in the other direction. This is where 95% of actors will try another technique until that one gets hard, and then they will try another and then another. (Sounds like many marriages.) When this kind of actor says, "Oh, I did that technique, it didn't work for me." That's not true. That actor never really did the technique. He merely dipped his toe into the water and decided swimming wasn't for him.

In running from one technique to another and another and another, the actor will never learn a way of working, he will never arrive at "life itself."

People use the word commitment casually. It is the easiest word in the English language to say and the hardest to do.

❖❖❖

Major acting key:

In every respect, acting is an act of commitment.

❖❖❖

Major acting key:

The word "casual" has no part in the world of acting.

❖❖❖

B.

The academic machine.

I have trained hundreds of acting teachers in my teacher

training program, wonderful and gifted teaching artists from around the world. This is one my favorite things I get to do, I love working with teachers.

These are simply my observations...

Most actor training in our country happens in the academic setting, high schools and colleges.

To attract students to actor training programs in the academic world, many schools employ a strategy I call the "smorgasbord" approach.

Just like having a bit of shrimp over here and some marinated cucumber salad over there, the smorgasbord approach to training actors is when a student gets a little taste of a whole bunch of different acting techniques.

Two very big problems with the smorgasbord approach...

First, the students can not grasp or more importantly, they will never experience, what the acting exercises are ultimately leading to. Even if the initial exercises have some positive benefit for a student, the work is never fulfilled. At best, students leave with the thought, "That was interesting but I have no idea what I got out of it and I have no clue what to do with it." and then they move on to another class and a different technique.

The most important thing they did not get out of that class? A way of working.

Flash forward. The student graduates after four years, deeply in debt, or his parents are, and he leaves school not having learned to act. This is very, very sad. If this student wants to act professionally, he will now have to train in a professional studio. So what was that four years of college actor training about?

A few years ago, I held auditions for a play I was directing. There were two roles for college age actors. I saw hundreds of actors audition for these parts and 95% of them did not know how to approach a piece of text. When I looked at the resumes, 95% of them were recent graduates of college acting programs that offer a smorgasbord approach to the training of actors.

The second problem is that, many of the students who go through the smorgasbord approach leave the college with the attitude, "Oh, Adler? Yeah, I did that in college, it's not for me." or "Oh, Meisner? Yeah, we did that in my school. It's not for me." The truth is, the student never really "did" the technique, how could he possibly know if it is "for him" or not?

It's like the story of the blind men and the elephant:

It was six men of Brooklyn,
To learning much inclined,
Who went to see the Elephant
(Though all of them were blind),
That each by observation
Might satisfy his mind.

The First approach'd the Elephant,
And happening to fall
Against his broad and sturdy side,
At once began to bawl:
"God bless me! but the Elephant

Is very like a wall!"

The Second, feeling of the tusk,
Cried, -"Ho! what have we here
So very round and smooth and sharp?
To me 'tis mighty clear,
This wonder of an Elephant
Is very like a spear!"

The Third approach'd the animal,
And happening to take
The squirming trunk within his hands,
Thus boldly up and spake:
"I see," -quoth he- "the Elephant
Is very like a snake!"

The Fourth reached out an eager hand,
And felt about the knee:
"What most this wondrous beast is like
Is mighty plain," -quoth he,-
"'Tis clear enough the Elephant
Is very like a tree!"

The Fifth, who chanced to touch the ear,
Said- "E'en the blindest man
Can tell what this resembles most;
Deny the fact who can,
This marvel of an Elephant
Is very like a fan!"

The Sixth no sooner had begun
About the beast to grope,
Then, seizing on the swinging tail
That fell within his scope,

"I see," -quoth he,- "the Elephant
Is very like a rope!"

And so these men of Brooklyn
Disputed loud and long,
Each in his own opinion
Exceeding stiff and strong,
Though each was partly in the right,
And all were in the wrong!

MORAL,

So, oft in opinion wars
The disputants, I ween,
Rail on in utter ignorance
Of what each other mean;
And prate about an Elephant
Not one of them has seen!

❖❖❖

Another problem in academic acting programs arises when beginning students are permitted to be in shows before they have strengthened their skills. The result of this endeavor only encourages any bad habits and theatrical notions the students might have. Selling tickets, keeping parents happy and being able to promote the acting program on the website are the priority rather than providing a cocoon for students where they have the space and time for metamorphosis and transformation. What a short sighted approach to actor training. Where are the leaders who care enough to protect the students from the pressures of performance before they are ready?

❖❖❖

Please be aware that there are acting classes comprised of inhuman exercises and mysterious, complex concepts and theories. These classes will get your mind spinning and your eyes crossing. You will leave each class stuck in your head and unable to act. The parts of you that need to be liberated and expressed will become restricted, constrained and paralyzed.

❖❖❖

There are acting teachers who relish arguing about acting techniques - bashing the ones they don't teach and defending the ones they do - and in almost every case, the teachers who are most vocal in their criticism of other techniques, have never really done them. This is called:

"Contempt prior to investigation."

It's a depressing, waste of time.

If you happen to run into this kind of teacher, run my friend, run.

C.

Every year, thousands of people get the idea that they should be an actor. Many of these thousands are attracted to the notion of acting because the great actors make it look like they are not doing anything, that acting requires nothing more than a good personality. There is also the fantasy of living the celebrity lifestyle.

If these people happen to attend a real acting class, they quickly discover that the work requires a willingness to be uncomfortable. So, for anyone who was looking for celebrity rather than learning a craft, a real acting class will naturally weed them out.

Chapter Three.

Acting Technique: Who cares?

Some people love to sit around and talk about technique. Of course, none of this chatter means anything until you actually get on your feet and do the work. Do it, then you will know.

In the professional world, no one cares what technique you studied. The only thing anyone cares about in the professional world is what you bring to the project. Every real director wants creative artists on the team, they do not want to know what you did back in acting class.

I have a strong recommendation. When you get a professional gig, do your work, do not talk about your technique, just do your work. Be the hardest working person in the room. Let your work speak for you. Make this a practice. Let the others talk about technique, you do your work.

Chapter Four.

Acting Technique: Where is it supposed to get you?

You may wonder, "What's at the end of acting technique?"

If you study a great acting technique with all of your heart and soul, all of your mind, all of your physical endurance. If you commit to it one hundred percent...

Where is it supposed to get you?

It is absolutely true that there is one ultimate place you must arrive in your acting if you are going to be what I have been calling a creative artist. It is the hardest thing to put into words, yet it is important to grapple with, to describe, and even though you can't see it or put your finger on it, you know it exists because you see how it manifests. It's as real as the ground you stand on.

You also know it exists because as a human organism, you are the living, breathing example of it.

Let me paint a picture for you...

- Schools of fish swim in formation, a massive synchronized aquatic organism turning on a dime. How in the world do they do it? You can read thousands of scientific studies, theory after theory, all leading up to one basic answer. No one knows.

- What is the built in biological clock in Monarch butter-flies that combines with magnetic fields, light sensitive molecules and the position of the sun to lead them on an epic 3000 mile journey called one of the most remark-able natural phenomena on the planet. How do they do it? No one really knows.

- They say there was this thing called the Big Bang. Ok, cool. But what was before the bang? A singularity? Come on, no one knows.

- They say the universe is still expanding. Expanding into what? Nobody knows.

- What is that thing we call space? There sure is a lot of it. They call it dark matter. Ok, what's dark matter? It's a great term for the simple truth, represented by this mathematical equation:

Dark matter = No one knows

- Planet earth was once a hot little rock until these smart little organisms crawled out of the sea and figured out that they could take an energy from 93 million miles away and turn it into an environment that would sustain life. How'd they do that? No one knows.

- What keeps us from flying off into outer space when we get out of the bed in the morning? They call it "gravity." What's that? Clearly, nobody knows.

- And that sun, she keeps burning away. What was the original spark that got her going? Come on, no one really knows.

- Of course, we have the greatest story known to mankind, the sperm meets the egg. Lot's of science about that encounter. Two meet up and become one and Bob's your uncle, we have life itself. Wait a minute, let's pause... did you really hear that? We have this thing called life itself. What is it, where did it come from, how is it possible? My friend, no one knows.

Let's look at "no one knows.".

Everything I have just mentioned lives in the space I call, "not knowing." We can also call it, "the mystery," or, "the unseen" and like the remarkable phenomena of the monarch butterflies, it is all completely natural and interconnected.

❖❖❖

Let me plant a seed with the following key...

MAJOR ACTING KEY:

Acting is much more about that which is unseen than that which is seen.

(This will become very clear when we get to the chapter on acting component number two.)

❖❖❖

The creative zone. We might describe it as being in the flow. The flow of what? The flow of life itself.

Great athletes talk a lot about this thing called "the zone," or being in "the flow."

Although the flow itself can't be seen, we can observe how it manifests and there are common experiences all athletes describe when it occurs:

- Complete absorption in the activity, nothing else seems to matter.
- Clarity of intention and a deep state of attention.
- Full involvement with the task at hand.
- Overflowing energy.
- Crowd noise, opponent reactions, and other distractions don't get in the way.
- The focus of attention is clearly on the task at hand.
- No self-consciousness. The ego is lost in the activity itself.
- No worry that things might not go well.
- Pure enjoyment in the activity itself without seeking any reward.
- Perception of time is transformed and doesn't matter.
- Everything suddenly becomes effortless.

Don't those eleven observations sound absolutely compelling and delicious when you imagine how you would like to experience your acting?

Let's continue...

Practitioners of a healing art called, Jin Shin Jyutsu, speak about the "flow of life," based on the physio-philosophy that energy pathways feed life into all of our cells and that these pathways can become blocked or stagnant causing harm to the organism.

Using their fingers on the patient, the practitioner of Jin Shin Jyutsu "listens" to the pulse which has all the information about what the person receiving the treatment needs.

A few years ago, my wife trained with a master Jin Shin Jyutsu teacher. In one session, as the participants were learning the pressure points, one student, who had her fingers on another student playing the role of the patient, asked the teacher, "How do I know if the pulse is the patients pulse or my own pulse?" The teacher replied very simply, "One pulse."

Please take that one in, the teacher called it:

"One pulse"

This is a profound phrase, "one pulse" and it is pointing to the fact that everything we know is in relationship. There is nothing that is not in relationship. We just forget.

When you walk through the woods, you see the trees and flowers and everything above the ground. Under the ground, there is a vast network of roots talking with each other, united in a singular mission, the survival of our planet. This is the real world wide web.

❖❖❖

Again, the question of this chapter:

"Acting Technique. Where is it supposed to get you?"

The answer:

Acting technique is supposed to point you towards the creative act. Another word I use for the creative act and for life itself is "It."

Basic math:

Creative Act/Life Itself = It

Ultimately, the artist must get out of the way so that "It" leads.

Your immediate question might be:

"How in the world do I do that? How do I get out of the way?"

Acting technique will not do it for you. What technique will do is strengthen you in ways that enable you to permit "It" to function as you unlock the gateway to the creation of life itself.

Sound big? It is.

And there's more...

Without any sort of acting training whatsoever, it is true that you might have a flash of true creativity and inspiration in a performance one night or in one take in front of the camera, but come tomorrow, you will be terrified that you might not ever reach that height again.

Technique will give you a way of working so that entering the creative zone is repeatable and so that you can count it.

Having arrived at this point of artistry and craft, you have nothing to worry about and this lack of tension makes your journey into the unknown richer, deeper and joyous.

Minnie Maddern Fiske, also known as "Mrs. Fiske", was called by many the most important American stage actress at the beginning of the 20th Century. She talked about this very thing...

"I like to remind myself that there can be, that there is, a complete technique of acting. Great acting, of course, is a thing of the spirit; in its best state is a conveyance of certain abstract spiritual qualities, with the person of the actor as medium. It is with this medium our art deals, with its slow, patient perfection as an instrument. The eternal and immeasurable accident of the theater which you call genius, that is a matter of the soul.

But with every genius I have seen, there was always the last word in technical proficiency. The inborn, mysterious something in these players can only inspire. It cannot be imitated. No school can make a Duse. But with such genius as hers has always gone a supreme mastery of the art of acting, a precision of performance so satisfying that it continually renews our hope and belief that acting can be taught.

43

Any one may achieve on some rare occasion an outburst of genuine feeling, a gesture of imperishable beauty, a ringing accent of truth; but the artist as actor knows how he did it. He can repeat it again and again and again. He can be depended on. Once he has thought out his role and found the means to express his thought, he can always remember the means.

And just as a master pianist may play with a different fire on different nights, but always strikes the same keys, so the skilled actor can use himself as a finely keyed instrument and thereon strike what notes he will. With due allowance for the varying mood and interest, the hundredth performance is as good as the first; or, for obvious reasons, far better. Genius is the great unknown quantity. Technique supplies a constant for the problem."

❖❖❖

the silverberg approach

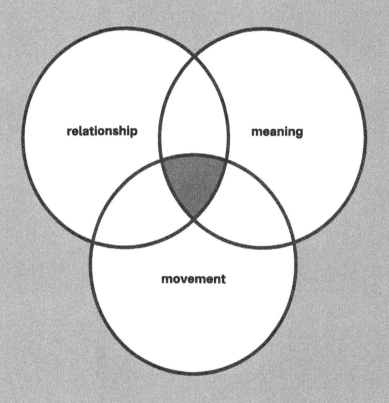

relationship

meaning

movement

LARRY SILVERBERG

the silverberg approach

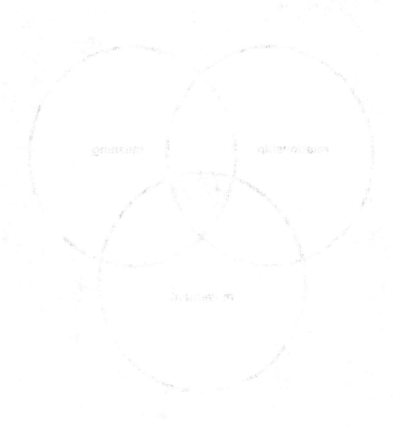

LARRY SILVERBERG

PART TWO. THE SILVERBERG APPROACH

Chapter Five.

The 3 Components of Acting.

Can we start with a fresh slate, a blank canvas?

I ask that you put aside common acting technique lingo, things like actions, objectives, beats, picking up your cues, pace, projection, blocking, etc. You don't have to throw anything away, just let it all sit over there on the table where you can pick it up later if you think it will be useful.

After teaching for many years, directing professionally around the country, writing many books on acting, working with thousands of actors at all levels of experience from every part of the world and from every training background...

I have absolute clarity that the art and craft of acting is made of just three simple components. Three, that's all.

The three components of acting are completely human and natural; they already live in you.

Most people have put these facilities into hibernation as a result of the socialization process. As an actor in training, you must revive and reinvigorate these skills and to do this, you will first need to bring them to awareness because change and growth only happens out of awareness.

Please note, I am not addressing things like your physical conditioning, flexibility and endurance as well as working on your vocal instrument and your diction which are essential if your aim is to act professionally. How could an actor possibly leave these out? You would be surprised how many do.

The three primary components of acting.

Let's get to it.

Chapter Six.

Acting Component One: Relationship.

To begin an exploration of acting component one, here is my next major acting key. It will serve as a road map for you to become a top 5% actor.

Major Acting Key:

The life of your acting depends on your ability to be available to, and responsive to, everything that is actually happening, as it is happening.

Slow down a moment and read it one more time:

The life of your acting depends on your ability to be available to, and responsive to, everything that is actually happening, as it is happening.

Now take a look at the six elements built into this simple statement:

• The Life

- To Be Available
- To Be Responsive
- To Everything
- Actually Happening
- As It Is Happening

1. The Life

   Your job is to bring life to the stage and in front of the camera. Not the approximation or representation of life, but life itself.

2. To Be Available.

   You must be deeply sensitized to everything being given to you by your acting partners and everything that is happening in the world around you.

3. To Be Responsive

   You must respond spontaneously, instinctually and from your truthful point of view.

4. To Everything

   You must be adept, agile, aware and awake so that you can respond to everything that is coming your way.

5. Actually Happening

   You must receive and respond to what is really happening, not what you think should be happening or what you think worked in last night's performance or in the previous take or back in rehearsals.

6. As It Is Happening

When must you respond? Right now, right now, right now...

You must respond as an expression of your impulses rather than pausing to consider what a good response might be. By the time you figure it out, it is way too late.

One more time...

The life of your acting depends on your ability to be available to, and responsive, to everything that is actually happening, as it is happening.

When all six of the elements in this statement are functioning fully, you have earned a dependable way of entering the creative zone.

Let's move on.

Here is my definition of acting:

Acting is an art of authentic relationship.

A basic fact of existence in our universe is that nothing exists outside of relationship.

Parent and child, boss and employee, chiropractor and patient, a chef and his pots and pans, an anteater and the ants, the moon and the tides, the planets as they circle the sun, the bees and the flowers. Cut a magnet in half and you still have a north and south pole. I could go on with this list ad infinitum.

The Dalai Lama said this:

"Consider the following. We humans are social beings. We come into the world as the result of others' actions. We survive here in dependence on others. Whether we like it or not, there is hardly a moment of our lives when we do not benefit from others' activities. For this reason it is hardly surprising that most of our happiness arises in the context of our relationships with others."

Again:

Acting is an art of authentic relationship.

Let's jot down some words related to the 2 key parts of the phrase - authentic and relationship - and see what we get:

Authentic:

Pure, reliable, true, trustworthy, actual, dependable, faithful, legit, sure, trusty, valid, certain, for real, genuine, undeniable, truthful, unquestionable, honest.

Relationship:

Connection, communication, contact, rapport, bond, interconnection, intimacy, kinship, affinity, reciprocity, exchange, mutuality, interdependence, involvement.

Now, match up any two words, one from each group. For example:

- Pure connection.
- Honest communication.
- Genuine involvement.

If you are to become a top 5% actor, the very first thing you must do is strengthen the skills of authentic relationship.

In other words, you must encourage your ability:

- to be in pure connection with another human being.
- to communicate with utter honesty.
- to have a genuine involvement with other people and with the world around you.

To do this, you must recognize the two sides of the authentic relationship coin.

Chapter Seven.

The Authentic Relationship Coin - Side One: Availability.

The way I like to describe availability for the actor is "To listen with the ear of one's heart."

Imagine that for a moment.

To listen with the ear of one's heart.

Doesn't that sound like a deeply human endeavor?

To listen with the ear of one's heart.

Do you see how these words immediately suggest greater sensitivity, openness and an embracing of the world around you and the people you are with?

To listen with the ear of one's heart.

Can you see how much more useful this is than the typical commands you may have had shouted at you in an acting class, "Focus!", "Concentrate!", "Be Present!", "Get out of your head!"

Any teacher who tells you to "Focus!", "Concentrate!", "Be Present!", "Get out of your head!", is doing you no favor. To tell you to get out of your head only turns your attention inward, putting you more deeply in your head.

What about the biggest acting cliche of all, to "be present?" It's one of the most absurd things a teacher can have you try to do.

Think about it for a moment:

Question: When you are involved in going over what you think should have happened in the past or you obsess about things you wish might have happened in the past, where are you doing it?

Answer: In the present.

Question: When you are fantasizing about what you hope will happen in the future, where are you doing it?

Answer: In the present.

What's the point I am making?

The point is:

When you are stuck going over events from the past, or you are lost in daydreams about the future, you are doing it right now. You are in every moment living in the present. Where else could you possibly be?

You exist moment to moment, it is the basic nature of life itself.

Life itself only exists right now, everything else is outside the domain of reality. Welcome to the real world.

Breaking News:

You can give up all attempts to be in the present.

Did I hear you breathe a sigh of relief?

❖❖❖
Acting Key:

Acting, just like life itself, is an art of right now, right now, right now, right now, right now. Each right now is taking you to the next right now.

❖❖❖

Yet...

There is a challenge that must be addressed...

Here now is one of the most important words in the actors vocabulary and the very first thing an actor must do is to revive and reinvigorate it because without it, what I like to call "true acting" cannot occur.

The word is:

"Attention"

Attention is big, really big. It is the golden ticket to claim acting component one as your own.

Why is it so big?

Attention is big because, as opposed to what most people think, the source of life is not in your head, it is in the world around you.

And...

Attention is the source of authentic relationship so obviously, it must be of primary interest to the actor in training.

❖❖❖

Acting Key:

The actor can only enter the creative zone when his or her attention is 100% directed outward.

❖❖❖

ATTENTION:

Join me online for exploration & exercises: availability and attention.

www.trueactinginstitute.com/learn

❖❖❖

Another thing to note as you begin your attention practice. Although it will take some consistent hard work, ultimately you will reach the basic, fundamental truth about attention:

Attention takes no effort whatsoever.

Attention is in fact, effortless.

❖❖❖

Chapter Eight.

The Authentic Relationship Coin - Side Two: Responsiveness.

Remember, our aim throughout this book is to help you be what I call a top 5% actor. To get there, you must first become deeply attentive and available to the world around you. That was the first side of the coin.

And then what?

Then you must respond, the second side of the coin.

(Although I have given you the image of two sides of a coin, please note that "receiving and responding" are in a continual, beautiful dance with each other so there is actually no division other than for discussion purposes.)

Ok, you know that you must respond.

Respond how?

Spontaneously, impulsively and honestly.

Respond when?

Right now. This means you must be the continual expression of everything that is happening in you as it is happening.

What gets in the way?

In life, many things get in the way of you being a spontaneous responder.

In life, many things get in the way of you permitting your impulses to lead you.

In life, many things get in the way of you expressing yourself honestly.

Like what?

a. The fear of looking foolish.
b. The fear of sounding stupid.
c. The fear that the other person may not like what you say or do.
d. The fear that you will not be appropriate.
e. The fear that you will lose a friend.
f. The fear that you will lose a job.
g. The fear that you won't be accepted by the group.
h. The fear that you will do something embarrassing.
i. The fear that you will reveal that you are different than the way you have always presented yourself.
j. The fear that your opinions will be criticized.

And on and on and on...

Everyone of these, a through j, and many more, spring from one issue that is a major part of the human experience.

Know the word?

Here it is:

Control.

It is a very common understanding that most human beings spend a lot of their time trying to control things that they have no control over whatsoever. It is a common discussion, yet most people still do it anyway and they do it most of the time. This leads to a tremendous waste of energy, resulting in much worry and suffering.

Question:

Can you make someone fall in love with you?

When I've asked that question in workshops I have led around the globe, every single person says "No!"

When I ask this follow up question:

"Ever try to make someone fall in love with you?"

Every single person says "Yes!"

❖❖❖

It is useful to note that if you consider the most important things in your life, you become acutely aware that you have no control over them:

• The beating of your heart. It keeps on beating away. One day it won't beat any more. How much of your day do you spend controlling it?

• Digesting your food. How much work does it take to make sure that happens?

63

- Breathing. If I didn't mention it, would you have stopped to notice that your body keeps breathing without you worrying much about it?

- Seeing. Your eyes keep taking all those images of the world around you and sending them to your brain and the only time you even remember that you have eyes is when there is a problem with them.

- Going to the bathroom. Can you make yourself go to the bathroom? You can certainly strain and push or eat a lot of prunes and roughage, but no, you can't make yourself go.

- Going to sleep. Can you make yourself go to sleep? You can take some drugs, but no, you really can't make yourself go to sleep.

Let's reflect on this a bit:

How do you go to sleep?

Hold on, slow down, this is a really great question...

How do you go to sleep?

The answer is:

You allow it to happen.

Because you have no guarantee that once you fall asleep you will actually wake up again, permitting yourself to fall asleep requires a few important ingredients:

The first is trust. You trust that if you do fall asleep, things are going to work out okay.

The next is relaxing. When you trust that things will work out okay, you start to relax and it becomes easier to fall asleep.

Another is that you accept going into the unknown because all you know when you lie down in bed is that you might fall asleep. Everything that happens after that is totally unknown to you.

Be aware. It is very easy to assume that after you fall asleep at night, you will wake up sometime the following morning. After all, this is exactly what has happened almost every other time you have ever done it. But this assumption is a very big mistake. Have an idea why?

Even though you have fallen asleep at night and woken up the following morning many hundreds of times before, it would be a very big mistake to assume that when you go to sleep tonight the same thing will happen again.

This assumption takes you out of the reality of life.

The truth of life is that anything is possible.

❖❖❖

Major Acting Key:

An actor must never assume anything.

❖❖❖

This is important for me to highlight...

The truth of life is that anything is possible.

Isn't that why so many people will spend a lot of their hard earned cash on lottery tickets even though the chances of winning are so incredibly small?

The truth is that from the moment you get out of bed in the morning, everything that is about to happen in your life is totally unknown. It doesn't matter how well organized you are or how thoroughly you have your day planned out, your life is one big improvisation. Yet you still get out of bed! How cool is that!

Here are two major keys to top 5% acting.

❖❖❖

Major Acting Key:

The moment you step on stage or in front of the camera, anything is possible.

❖❖❖

Major Acting Key:

Embrace everything, deny nothing.

❖❖❖

Embrace everything, deny nothing. What a powerful phrase!

When you are in performance on stage and in front of the

camera, you must be willing and able to work with everything that comes your way. To work with everything rather than to work only with what you think should be happening or what you wish were happening.

To embrace everything, deny nothing.

What do you think this requires of you?

It requires just two simple things:

1. Your ability to be available to, and responsive, to everything that is actually happening, as it is happening. Sound familiar?

2. Giving up all control.

So how do you do this, how do you give up controlling when the habit is so deeply ingrained?

The answer is two fold.

The first part is that you must have the desire to do it. Sound simple? Yes, it is. You must have a strong desire to stop controlling all of those things you have no control over anyway.

The second part of the answer is awareness. You must become aware of your need to control everything and the actions you take to control everything and then, out of your desire, to let it all go.

How long will that take?

In the blink of an eye.

You can stop trying to control all of those things you really have no control over anyway right now.

Then, each time the old habit pulls at you and you find yourself trying to control everything again, you can let it all go again and again and again.

It's a practice.

The practice of giving up control.

❖❖❖

When you give up trying to control everything:

You permit life to happen

When you give up trying to control everything:

You allow you to happen.

When you give up trying to control everything:

Life becomes simpler. All of the energy that was drained out of you by your efforts to control everything will become available to you and you can put it to much better use - turning your life into a creative act.

This will carry over to your acting which will also become a creative act.

Take note:

• The creative act can not occur when you are in control.

- Life itself will not be available to you when you are in control.
- "It" can not lead when you are in control.

Can you give up trying to control everything?

Yes, you can.

The ability to live fully without trying to control everything is built into you as a human organism.

Flip that little control switch to the off position and you will suddenly find a whole new dimension of freedom, spontaneity and play. Sound good? It is.

❖❖❖

Chapter Nine.

Acting Component Two: Meaning.

How utterly simple.

Everything in your world has meaning to you.

It's your point of view.

It's how you "see" the world.

And...

It is the biggest piece of the acting puzzle that is missing in the majority of acting on a global basis.

In my teaching travels around the world, I have asked an important question to every group of professional actors, directors, acting teachers and acting students that I have worked with:

"How many times have you seen a play that has literally taken your breath away. Where you were so involved with the actors that you forgot you were sitting in a theatre surrounded by hundreds of people. Where what was happening on stage was so intimate and true, you felt like you were looking through a peephole that maybe you shouldn't be looking through?

I have asked this question to thousands of people and 95% of them told me that in their whole life, they have had this kind of transformative experience in a theatre just once or twice.

Unfortunate, don't you think?

There is no mystery here. We must trace the root cause of why so much theatre is so lifeless back to the acting classroom.

The basic acting concepts taught by almost every acting class in the world - objectives and actions - are mostly taught at the expense of anything that is going to help you really act.

These by rote phrases are being taught without an understanding or concern for the singular thing that makes them necessary in the first place.

What is that?

Hold on, it's coming...

❖❖❖

Here is one absolute acting class truth:

If a teacher asks an acting student to produce a result - smile more, be sadder, give me more energy, etc... - unless the acting student has a way of working that gets him to the genuine embodiment of those results, he has no choice but to push, to strain and to fake it.

95% of theatre is lifeless because so many acting classes

are demanding the students produce results that the students have no way of fulfilling truthfully. The students producing results by faking is then encouraged by the teacher and rewarded by getting cast in the show.

By the way, if a teacher or director tells you that they need "more energy," my friend, you are working with someone who is deeply out of touch with the craft of acting and they will not be able to help you in any way whatsoever.

This is why it is urgent and essential that you have a healthy, human way of working and very strong internal artistic values for the work you do.

❖❖❖

An objective is not theoretical, it is human.

An action is not theoretical, it is human.

The lack of understanding about basic life truths - how we function as human organisms and how to translate that to the craft of acting - has resulted in acting that is empty, hollow and without life itself.

And so actors are being encouraged to do one thing only. Here's how I say it:

❖❖❖

Actors are being trained to try to make it look like something is happening that is not really happening.

❖❖❖

Yes, in fact, 95% of the acting we see is nothing more than:

Trying to make it look like something is happening that is not really happening.

Another way to describe this is that actors are being encouraged:

To lie.

Whether it's to try to get a laugh or to try and be interesting or to try to get a good review, most acting is a series of one faked moment to the next faked moment to the next faked moment.

When you try to make it look like something is happening that is not really happening, there is:

- no true availability.
- no true responses.
- no true meaning.

Is it ok for an actor to lie to the audience?

When you go to have your teeth examined, is it okay with you if the dentist lies to you about the condition of your gums? Probably not.

So why would it be acceptable to go to the theatre and be lied to by the actors?

We are talking about acting component two, meaning:

- Meaning is your next step to enter the flow of true acting.
- Meaning is an intrinsic part of the creative zone.
- Meaning is the river of life that you must start swimming in when you act.

To be more specific.

What kind of meaning are we talking about?

We are talking about personal meaning.

Personal meaning is also completely unseen. We know that it lives in us. Where does it live in us? No one really knows.

When you think about someone you love, you know that love is real, yet if a doctor did heart surgery on you, would he see that love there? No, he wouldn't.

Now, we are illuminating the major acting key I gave you earlier:

"Acting is much more about that which is unseen than that which is seen."

Here are some beautiful words from John Gardner:

"Meaning is not something you stumble across, like the answer to a riddle or the prize in a treasure hunt. Meaning is something you build into your life.

You build it out of your own past, out of your affections and loyalties, out of the experience of humankind as it is passed on to you, out of your own talent and understanding, out of the things you believe in, out of the things and people you love, out of the values for which you are willing to sacrifice something.

The ingredients are there. You are the only one who can put them together into that unique pattern that will be your life.

Let it be a life that has dignity and meaning for you. If it does, then the particular balance of success or failure is of less account."

❖❖❖

Major Acting Key:

The actor's medium is personal meaning.

❖❖❖

Earlier, I told you:

"The basic acting concepts taught by almost every acting class in the world - objectives and actions - are mostly taught at the expense of anything that is going to help you really act. These by rote phrases are being taught without an understanding or concern for the singular thing that makes them necessary in the first place.

What is that?

Hold on, it's coming..."

❖❖❖

Now...

We are almost there.

First...

Let me expand a bit by adding one more item to the list.

It is not only objectives and actions that are taught at the expense of anything that is going to help you really act...

It is also, the very words of the script themselves.

The majority of acting students are being trained to focus on the words and how to deliver them. Place emphasis here, take a pause here, give an inflection there.

Let's talk about that one, inflection.

❖❖❖

To the dictionary:

inflection, noun, in·flec·tion: Changing the pitch, tone, or loudness of our words are ways we communicate meaning in speech, though not on the printed page. A rising inflection at the end of a sentence generally indicates a question, and a falling inflection indicates a statement, for example.

❖❖❖

Many acting students are being encouraged to use inflection

to communicate meaning that does not actually exist other than as an idea or a concept.

Here too we have another layer of "trying to make it look like something is happening that is not actually happening."

Or, we might say:

"Trying to make it sound like something is happening that is not actually happening."

❖❖❖

What about this part of the definition:

"A rising inflection at the end of a sentence generally indicates a question, and a falling inflection indicates a statement, for example."

Hmmmm.... Nice and pat as an idea but it is not a human reality. In human land, people talk in all kinds of ways and with all kinds of inflections.

For example, try this:

Say the following sentence out loud and raise your inflection at the end:

"I can ask you a question in many different ways, can't I?"

Now say the same sentence again but this time make your inflection go down at the end:

"I can ask you a question in many different ways, can't I?"

What's my point?

My point is that life itself does not care about the rules of inflection.

Life itself is much bigger than the rules of inflection.

It's the same with pauses.

Many directors love to get clever by having the actor pause to highlight a "special moment." They sit at home before rehearsals begin and diagram it all out in their script. Nice idea but what we end up seeing on that stage is an actor with big blank holes of nothingness interrupting the speaking of words which have no meaning.

These pauses are nothing more than:

"Trying to make it sound like something is happening that is not actually happening."

It's really very simple...

In life, the reason you pause when speaking is that for a variety of reasons, you suddenly find it impossible to speak. You don't decide to "do" a pause, we can say that "the pause is doing you."

The great mime, Marcel Marceau said:

"Do not the most moving moments of our lives find us without words?

❖❖❖

Ok, that was my expansion, let's get to it...

Here is the new, expanded version of the statement I gave you just a short while back:

The basic acting concepts taught by almost every acting class in the world - objectives, actions and the text - are mostly taught at the expense of anything that is going to help you really act.

Acting students are encouraged to focus on the words of the text in an intellectual, conceptual way which has no relationship to life itself.

All of this is being taught without an understanding or concern for the singular thing that makes the words, the objectives and the actions necessary in the first place.

❖❖❖

What is the singular thing that makes the words, the objectives and the actions necessary in the first place?

Here it is.

It is one word.

It is very, very simple.

The word is:

"Need."

I say it again.

Need.

This is another word that brings with it tremendous misunderstanding and the baggage of old cliches and theatricalized ways of working in the acting classroom and on the stage.

Let's get basic and human.

❖❖❖

Major Acting Key:

Everything you say and do must be purposeful.

❖❖❖

Everything you say and do must be purposeful.

This acting key is not theoretical, it is human, it is based on your life.

In life:

You do not say words, and you do not do the things you do, for no reason.

In life:

There is a purpose for all of your words and for all of your behavior.

In life:

From the moment you wake up, and all day long until you fall back asleep at night, your life is a series of behaviors, words, objectives and actions.

(We will get to this in greater specificity in the chapter on acting component three.)

The important thing to recognize right now is that in life:

Everything you say and do is purposeful.

And...

Everything you say and do springs from a deep seated need.

A deep seated need in who?

A deep seated need in you.

The word I like most for this need is:

Desire.

❖❖❖

Oh yes, what a beautiful word:

Desire.

❖❖❖

You have an unquenchable desire.

This desire drives you.

Here's a quote I love:

"What makes the engine go? Desire, desire, desire."

Your desire is the core of you. It is completely human. My own belief, for whatever this is worth, is that this desire was planted in you before you arrived and your whole life is the struggle to get closer to the fulfillment of it.

❖❖❖

I call this desire:

"The Deeper Wish"

I love this phrase.

Why?

I love the phrase "the deeper wish" because it implies that desire is:

1. Deep within you. It is completely personal, intimate and specific to you.
2. It is active. When you have a wish, you have to actually do something to fulfill it.

Another way to think of the deeper wish:

It is what your life is about.

Many people wonder:

"What is my life about?"

The answer is revealed when you discover:

Your deeper wish.

Your deeper wish is the unseen force, like gravity, that pulls at you as long as your heart is beating, whispering in your ear, speaking to you in your dreams.

It is important for you to bring to consciousness what your deeper wish is. For most people, it remains hidden but you are not most people. You want to act.

For you, the actor, it is essential to uncover your deeper wish and to see how everything you do, every action you take, can be traced back in one way or another to your deeper wish.

You may ask...

"Why is it so important to come to terms with my own deeper wish?"

Great question!

Here's why...

The character in the script also has a deeper wish. It was planted in the character before he or she arrived and it came from their maker, the writer.

And...

You must look at the character as a human being who is driven by a strong, deep seated need. Just like you.

84

And...

To play the role, you must understand the character's deeper wish and then you must literally step inside it. Only then will everything that the character says and everything that the character does make sense.

And...

Once you have adopted the deeper wish of the character, it gives you a way to navigate the circumstances of the play. Now, you will always know how close or how distant you are from accomplishing the essential thing you are there to fulfill.

That is the basis of all dramatic literature.

Every character is on a mission to fulfill their deeper wish. This endeavor is urgent and the stakes are high.

The same is true for every human organism. They just forget.

❖❖❖

Again, my question was:

Why is it so important to come to terms with your own deeper wish?

By figuring out your own deeper wish and seeing it as the guiding force in your life, you will then have a human way to do the very same thing with the character in the script.

❖❖❖

I have a profoundly useful way for you to uncover your deeper wish.

To do the deeper wish exercise with me, go to this link:

www.trueactinginstitute.com/learn

Here is the most vital part of the deeper wish story when it comes to acting. It is not enough to know what the deeper wish of the character is, you must then make that deeper wish your deeper wish.

Listen to this one more time:

You must know what the deeper wish of the character is and then you must make it your own.

Very Big, Highlighted, Key Point...

Unless you make the need of the character your need, you have not earned the right to stand on that stage.

I am going to say this again.

Very Big, Highlighted, Key Point...

Unless you make the need of the character your need, you have not earned the right to stand on that stage.

❖❖❖

Here is how I began this chapter:

Acting Component Two: Meaning.

How utterly simple.

Everything in your world has meaning to you.

It's your point of view.

It's how you "see" the world.
And...

It is the biggest piece of the acting puzzle that is missing in the majority of acting on a global basis.

❖❖❖

Why is "meaning" the biggest piece of the acting puzzle that is missing in the majority of acting on a global basis? Here's why.

Meaning is the biggest piece of the acting puzzle that is missing in the majority of acting on a global basis because most acting classes, and the actors they train, leave out the crucial other word.

Remember?

Yes, they leave out:

Personal.

Remember the actor's medium?

Yes, it's:

Personal meaning.

Please see how simple this is and how much sense it makes.

When you do things in life, you have a true need to do them. This need is based on things that are meaningful to you.

If you ask someone to marry you, you have a real need to do that. If you get asked to marry someone and you say yes, you have a real need to do that.

And...

When the character does things in the script, he or she has a real need to do those things too.

But...

When you first get the script and you read the part you are going to play, you do not have the real need to do the things the character is doing.

And...

By opening night or by the time you shoot the scene, you must have taken the character's need and made it your own.

Again...

By opening night or by the time you shoot the scene, you must have taken the character's need and made it your own.

Yet...

This is what most actors leave out.
And you know why, right?

Yes, they don't make the character's need their own because what they are doing is this:

"Trying to make it look and sound like something is happening that is not actually happening."

Remember that one?

Yes...

Trying to make it look and sound like something is happening that is not actually happening is not acting, it is not even related to acting.

❖❖❖

The big effort of rehearsals has a lot to do with making the need of the character your need so that by the time opening night arrives or by the time you shoot the scene, you have a true purpose to say the things you say and a true purpose to do the things you do.

Wow!

When this is happening it is a very big wow.

Now...

Everything you do on that stage or in front of that camera will be necessary.

Necessary to who?

Necessary to you!

Now you do not have to pretend to need to do what you are doing because...

You actually need to do it!

Wow!

And...

When you have the true need to speak the words of the script and do the things you have to do, you can trust that it will be communicated to the audience and reach them "where they live."

Now, you have earned your right to stand on that stage.

Now, you have earned your right to stand in front of that camera.

Now, you can trust that the meaning you have injected inside everything you say and do will be communicated to the audience and reach them "where they live."

This is exciting.

Acting becomes exciting for you to do and exciting for the audience to witness.

Now, you no longer have to worry if you are "entertaining" them enough.

The only actor who worries if he is "entertaining" them enough is the actor who works without meaning and has no true purpose to stand on the stage or in front of the camera.

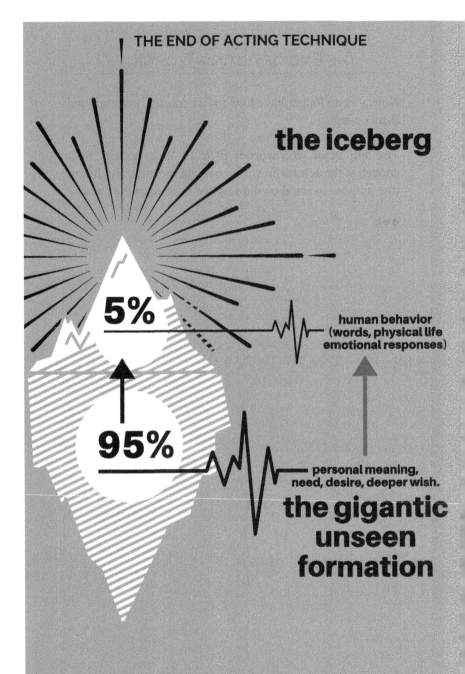

the iceberg

5%

human behavior
(words, physical life
emotional responses)

95%

personal meaning,
need, desire, deeper wish.

the gigantic
unseen
formation

LARRY SILVERBERG

I have a really good diagram for you. It's an iceberg. The iceberg diagram illustrates our conversation about personal meaning.

In life, all human behavior, including words, physical life and emotional responses, do not come from no where.

Before all words, physical life and emotional responses, there is personal meaning, need, desire and the deeper wish at the core.

When you talk with someone, or when you observe someone's behavior, you are seeing an external manifestation of a deeply personal, unseen process.

When you honestly observe your own words and actions, you will see that they are the result of a deeply personal process unseen to the world around you and known only by you.

The words, physical life and emotional responses are always the last thing to occur. These are just 5% of the story.

Before words, physical life and emotional responses, there is some "baking and brewing" going on down in that "furnace" of yours. This is 95% of the story.

Eventually...

All of that baking and brewing will bubble up to the surface and the world will observe your words, physical life and emotional responses.

I call this "baking and brewing", the "gigantic unseen formation."

As an actor, you must spend a great deal of your time working with the gigantic unseen formation.

Why?

Because the gigantic unseen formation will result in words, physical life and emotional responses that are necessary and true.

Just like in life!

This is exactly what I mean when I say that you must make the need of the character your need.

You do it so that...

Everything you say and everything you do on stage and in front of the camera is necessary and true.

❖❖❖

You might be asking...

"How?"

"How do I make the character's need my own?"

Another great question.

The answer comes in the form of a process I call:

"Personalizing the point of view of the character."

This is a beautiful process with profound results in your acting.

94

I can teach this to you in my online classroom.

Join me online for exploration & exercises: The art of personalization.

www.trueactinginstitute.com/learn

Chapter Ten.

What's the story, Jerry?

Let's take a few moments for a brief review.

It is my belief that you can be a top 5% actor.

It is a belief based on the fact that when you start to address the 3 simple acting components, you will immediately raise the quality of your acting above what the other 95% of actors are doing.

❖❖❖

Acting is a human event, it is not technical. Let's leave the theories and concepts of acting to people who like to spend their time arguing about all that.

While they argue, we have work to do.

The craft of acting, although quite challenging, is simple. There is no mystery to it. It makes sense because you already live it.

❖❖❖

Acting is an act of commitment.

And...

The basis of all dramatic literature is conflict.

Plays and screenplays are about characters who must struggle to accomplish something against all odds.

So when you play a role, the bottom line is that you are on a mission.

Another way to say this is:

You are there to solve a very big problem.

And...

Your commitment will be tested.

Some characters in the story will make things difficult for you, while others will help you succeed.

You will also go through the most intense internal conflicts. (Look at Frodo in *The Lord of the Rings* or Neo in *The Matrix*, two great examples.)

The circumstances of the play make things tough on you. To accomplish your mission, you will face many hardships.

Did I hear you say that sounds like life?

Think about it this way:

If you play golf and you know that every time you get up to hit the ball you are going to get a hole in one:

1. Would it be very interesting for the crowd to watch?

No, of course not.

2. Would it be interesting for you to do?

No, of course not.

3. Would you have any sense of satisfaction or fulfillment after hitting the hole in one?

No, of course not.

We know that accomplishing something is only interesting and only leads to great satisfaction when it is difficult to do.

Take note:

Look at the way children play. They make things harder not easier. The fun is in the effort to overcome the obstacles. If a child rides a skateboard, do they want a nice, neat, level pavement? No! They want really hard ramps and slopes and kickers to do their skateboard tricks.

If things come too easy, like hitting that hole in one every time, it will be of no interest to you.

If what you are doing on stage is easy, meaning an imitation of what has been done before, it will be of no interest to you.

If it is of no interest to you, it will be of no interest to the audience.

This is why when you go to a play and you look around the audience during the show, you see so many people sleeping in their seats or texting or looking at Facebook.

You may wonder...

"If acting is human, what is the difference between my life and my acting?"

One difference is that acting requires you:

"To be natural on purpose."

Hah!

How do you do that?

Reflect on the discussion we had about "it."

To be natural on purpose, you must enter the "creative zone", you must be in "the flow", you must permit "it" to lead.

But...

This is exactly where 95% of actors are stuck in their heads.

What are they doing up there in their heads?

They are:

"Trying to make it look and sound like something is happening that is not actually happening."

This is a lie.

Take note:

The audience always knows when they are being lied to. They may not always know consciously but when they leave the theatre, they will have forgotten about the show by the time the waiter places the meatloaf on the table.

❖❖❖

Acting is an art of authentic relationship.

Relationship, not the thoughts in your head, is the source of life itself.

This requires you to revive your ability to give another person and the world around you your complete attention.

To listen with the ear of your heart.

This means that you must become deeply available to "over there" rather than the acquired habit of placing most of your attention on yourself.

When your attention is on yourself, you can only work with the same three characters in every play or movie that you act in.

Know their names?

You will see their names on the first page of every script you are handed.

Their names are "Me, Myself and I."

❖❖❖

As you are honing your skills of availability, you must also begin to permit yourself to respond to what is being given to you by your acting partners and by the world around you.

Respond how?

Spontaneously, impulsively and honestly.

Respond when?

Right now.

There are many things that get in the way of you doing this, but it all boils down to one fundamental issue:

Control.

You must give up control.

To do this it is useful to bring to awareness all the things you try to control that you actually have no control over whatsoever.

You have a great model for not controlling everything.

Here it is:

The most important things in your life are happening without you trying to control them, they happen naturally, without effort and most of the time, you give them no thought at all.

Like falling asleep.

To fall asleep, you relax and trust it will all work out. You easily head into the unknown of sleep. You permit it to happen.

Giving up control is one of the requirements of true acting.

Giving up control will take you on a fast track towards the creative act.

Giving up control will get you out of the way so that "it" can function.

Quite often (95% of the time), text, objectives and actions are taught without any regard for the most essential acting ingredient:

Personal meaning.

Without personal meaning, the words of the script will remain hollow and lifeless.

Without personal meaning, the objectives will remain academic and barren.

Without personal meaning, the actions will remain formularized and vapid.

In life, your days are filled with words, objectives and actions too.

And...

Your words, objectives and actions do not come from no-where.

You do not speak or do the things you do for no reason.

So where do your words, objectives and actions spring from?

Simple.

Need.

You have a need.

A deep seated need.

You have a "deeper wish" that is driving you.

It is "what your life is about."

And so...

Everything you do is purposeful.

The same is true on stage.

The character you play also has a deeper wish.

You must step inside the character's deeper wish.

Why?

Because...

Everything you say and everything you do on stage must be purposeful.

This means that when you play the role:

You must have an authentic need to speak the words and to do the things you do.

Whose need must you have?

Your need.

To be clear.

If your name is Jerry, you must have Jerry's need.

❖❖❖

Rehearsals are the time where you get to make the character's need your need.

So Jerry must make the character's need Jerry's need.

The two must become one.

This is called personalization.

When you have done this, you have earned your right to stand on that stage.

This is a very big wow!

❖❖❖

Chapter Eleven.

Acting Component Three: Movement.

A basic fact:

Everything that is alive moves.

Even inside your body, there's a lot of stuff moving around all the time.

Nothing that is alive stands still.

Look at a photo of you as an infant.

It is obvious that as a human organism, you were built to evolve.

Movement:

It is a basic hallmark of life itself.

You are a movement machine.

Let's dive in...

You wake up and it begins.

Your whole day will be a series of what I call "doings."

One doing after another, all day, every day.

What is a "doing?"

Simple.

A doing is something you do.

But not just "anything" you do.

No.

Then what?

A doing is something specific you do.

That's your life.

Your life is made up of a series of "specific" things you do.

One after another.

And...

Each one of these specific things that you do, you do for...

A specific reason.

Wait...

Hold on a moment here.

Where do they spring from do you imagine, these specific doings?

What are they the manifestation of?

Slow down and think back...

Yes...

Every specific thing you do is a result of a need. The need motivates you to do something specific to satisfy this need.

And...

Every need and every doing can be traced back to the core of who you are, remember that one?

Yes...

Your deeper wish, what your life is about.

❖❖❖

"Doings"

I love that word because it is human.

You can certainly do what you'd like, but I have thrown out the old acting technique lingo, objectives and actions.

It's not the fault of the two words, it is that...

Many acting classes are not teaching their students that objectives and actions are not technical, they are not a formula, they are human, they are modeled after how human beings function.

To be utterly clear:

Human beings, in every moment, are doing something specific for a specific reason.

Think about it this way, your life looks like this:

You do one specific thing for a specific reason.

Followed by,

You do one specific thing for a specific reason.

Followed by,

You do one specific thing for a specific reason.

Followed by,

You do one specific thing for a specific reason.

Followed by,

You do one specific thing for a specific reason.

And on and on and and on.

So, in your acting...

If there is any moment on stage or in front of the camera that you are not doing something specific for a specific reason, you are no longer acting.

We could also say it this way:

If there is any moment on stage or in front of the camera that you are not doing something specific for a specific reason, you are doing something unrelated to acting.

Here's a simple example. Imagine this:

- You have to go to work.

- It's Thursday and you have to be at work at 9 a.m., in 45 minutes.

- You are choosing clothes to wear today.

- You have a meeting with your boss at 9:15 a.m.

- You set up this meeting with your boss one month ago.

- You requested to meet with him to ask him for a significant raise and a Christmas sales bonus.

- Your bills, and your debt, have been piling up. Your credit cards are maxed out.

- Your daughter has been accepted into college and a first deposit due date is approaching.

- Your daughter applied to ten schools and this school was the only one she was invited to attend.

- If you get the raise and bonus, you will have enough money to pay the school deposit and within a few months, you will be able to cover her first year at school. Paying the credit cards off can wait.

Now, knowing all of this...

Do you imagine that the attention you give to choosing the outfit to wear to work today will be different than on any other day?

Yes, of course it will.

This is the basic construction of all dramatic literature:

The day we meet the characters is not "any" day in their lives, it is always the "most special" day in their lives.

How does it work, this thing called "the doing?"

I have a short scene for you to read. To set up the scene, here are the circumstances that you would know had you read the entire play:

- The characters are Darlene and Harry.

- The scene you are about to read is their second date.

- Darlene and Harry are in their early fifties.

- Darlene and Harry have never been married.

- Darlene works on a pillow manufacturing assembly line and Harry is a traveling salesman.

- Darlene spends most of her nights eating too much ice cream and watching the Hallmark channel. Harry sits in bars alone and drinks too much.

- Their first date went really well, they made a nice connection. She invited Harry to come to her place the next night for a home cooked meal.

- Darlene thinks Harry is finally "the one" for her.

- Harry thinks that he might have finally met the girl for him.

Here's the scene.

Harry and Darlene are sitting in her kitchen eating the meal she prepared.

❖❖❖

Harry: This is really a super meal you made for me Darlene, I didn't expect it.

Darlene: Like I said, I burned the biscuits and over cooked the chicken.

Harry: Come on Darlene, please don't cry, I love crisp, I just love it.

Darlene: Crisp is one thing but dried out and tough is another.

Harry: Look at me, I'm on my third helping here and this sauce is amazing and I ain't kidding around!

Darlene: It's from a can.

Harry: But boy do you know how to put it all together, not everyone's got a knack for that.

Darlene: Got it from my mother I guess.

Harry: Look at me, I'm lickin' my fingers over here, Darlene, cleaning every little crumb it's so good.

❖❖❖

First things first.

You know the circumstances prior to the scene because I gave them to you.

Now...

What's going on in the scene?

Where do we find the answer?

Simple:

It's in the text.

The text is your bible.

❖❖❖

Major Acting Key.

Every choice you make must be based on the information you get from the text. If you can not show how the text led you to your choice, you have no right to that choice.

❖❖❖

From the scene, we know:

- Darlene burned the biscuits and overcooked the chicken.

- Darlene is quite upset about the results of her cooking.

- Harry is eating the food and is trying very hard to get Darlene to believe that he likes it.

Simple, yes?

Yes, it is.

❖❖❖

My next question for you:

As you read the scene and look at Harry's words and behavior, what would you say is his "doing?"

It is very clear that Harry, with everything he says and does, is trying to make Darlene feel better.

One way you could say "the doing" is that Harry is making an attempt -

"To encourage her."

Another way you might say the doing is that Harry is trying -

"To lift her spirits."

Let's say you decide to work with the first doing:

"To encourage her."

Now...

You are playing the role of Harry.

You know what your doing is. It is "to encourage her."

Now what do you do?

Simple.

You do it.

You do the doing.

Important question.

Who do you do the doing with?

Answer:

You do the doing with your partner. You try it on for size when you work with the other actor.

This is not how 95% of actors are working.

95% of actors name their "action" and then they go home and figure out how to "play" the action.
They call it "tactics"

When applied to the craft of acting, "tactics" is one of the most destructive and misguided words in the English language. It sounds like a bunch of generals sitting around the war room planning a battle.

To illuminate why tactics, and the way they are being taught are so absurd and spurious, here is a questions for you.

Question:

When an actor goes home and figures out his tactics, (how he will play the action,) what is the most important ingredient in the entire acting experience he is leaving out?

Answer:

When an actor goes home and figures out his tactics, he is leaving out-

THE OTHER PERSON. THE ACTING PARTNER.

When an actor goes home and figures out his tactics, and then brings what he figured out to the rehearsal and does his tactics, the other person might as well not even be there.

Here we have another primary reason that 95% of theatre is devoid of life.

Actors are being trained to figure out their tactics at home and then to "do it on" the other person.

This is not acting.
This is not related to acting.

How you work on the "doing" is very simple.

It is completely human.

First:

Know what the doing is.

Next:

Get together with your acting partner.

And then:

Do the doing.

You may ask:

"How do I do the doing?"

Great question!

Answer:

You don't have to know "how" to do the doing.

You will discover "how" to do the doing as you are doing it.

❖❖❖

Major Acting Key.

You must discover how to do the doing in the doing of it rather than in the thinking about it.

❖❖❖

And...

As you are working with your partner and you are doing the doing...

Your partner will give you the "how" to do it.

Wonderful!

Again:

You only have to know the "what"

Your partner gives you the "how"

❖❖❖

Pop Quiz Question!

In this way of working -

- You only have to know the "what"

- Your partner gives you the "how"

it is required that you have the ability to be IN A WHAT with your acting partner?
Answer:

In this way of working -

- You only have to know the "what" (the doing)

- Your partner gives you the "how" (how to do it)

it is required that you have the ability to be IN AN AUTHENTIC RELATIONSHIP with your acting partner.

You see? There it is. Acting component one: Relationship.

I love this!

Simply by being deeply available to your partner, as you "do the doing", your partner will give you the roadmap for how to do it.

When you are actually available, in every moment, your partner will reveal to you if you are getting:

- closer to

- or further from

accomplishing the doing.

❖❖❖

For example...

Let's go back to the scene with Harry and Darlene.

You are playing Harry and your doing is "to encourage her." At one point in the scene, you have to say this line:

"Come on Darlene, please don't cry, I love crisp, I just love it."

Obviously, from the text, we know that Darlene is distraught and she is crying.

Imagine that right as you say the words, "please don't cry" you follow your impulse to reach over and put your hand on your acting partners cheek to comfort her.

Now imagine that the actress playing Darlene cries even harder, gets up from the table and goes to the sink, turning away from you. Maybe you go over and whisper to her gently, tenderly, "I love crisp, I just love it."

Here's a different possibility...

Imagine again that right as you say the words, "please don't cry" you follow your impulse to reach over and put your hand on your acting partners cheek to comfort her.

What if this time the actress playing Darlene puts her hand over yours and then takes your hand and kisses it?

Well now you might discover yourself pulling her hand to your mouth and give it a kiss as you say the words, "I love crisp, I just love it."

Wow!

There was no pre-planning for any of this, it was all discovered as you worked together, each one of you leading the other person to the discovery of how to do the doing.
Wait!

Believe me dear friend, the discovery of this kind of beautiful, unexpected and alive moments are light years beyond anything you might have come up with by figuring out your tactics at home by yourself.

Basic mathematics:

Figuring out tactics at home by yourself = technical, cliche and without life.

Discovering how to do the doing as you do it with your partner = Unexpected, human and alive.

Here is the next urgent and essential basic ingredient of true acting.

It is simple and the majority of human beings do it all the time naturally and without giving it a thought.

To introduce this ingredient, let's use the example I used earlier when I had you playing the role of Harry.

Once again...

Imagine that right as you say the words, "please don't cry" you follow your impulse to reach over and put your hand on your acting partner's cheek to comfort her.

Now imagine that the actress playing Darlene cries even harder, gets up from the table and goes to the sink, turning away from you.

Consider this:

If placing your hand on the cheek of the actress playing Darlene resulted in her crying even harder and running to the sink and turning away from you...

Do you think that you will get up, go over to her and put your hand on her cheek again?

Of course not!

In my example, here's how you responded to her behavior:

"You go over and whisper to her gently, tenderly, "I love crisp, I just love it."

Do you know what the word is for what you just did?

It is one of the most important words in the actors vocabulary.

The word is:

"Adjust"

Simple, right?

Yes, it is.

It is one of the most important words in the actors vocabulary and yet, 95% of actors cannot do it.

In life...

People do it all the time.

The only people I see not doing it are actors.

Consider this:

Along with many other drivers on the highway, you are driving at 80 miles per hour in a 65 miles per hour zone.

Then, a state trooper gets on the road.

What does everyone do?

Yes, everyone slows down.

Everyone "adjusts."

Then the state trooper gets off at the exit.

What does everyone do?

Everyone speeds up to 80 again.

It's called adjusting.

Consider this one:

You are on a long line at the grocery store, waiting to pay the cashier.

Then, a new cashier lane opens up two lanes down. What do you and a few other people do?

You all zoom over to the newly available lane.

It's called adjusting.

Most people do it very naturally and without thought.

The only people I see not adjusting are actors. But when you practice your tactics at home and then do your tactic on the other person, there is no relationship, there is no adjusting and there is no life.

Riffing off of our discussion on movement, let's review how I describe the combination of elements that lead to a vibrantly alive performance. It will be good to hear this one again.

And...

If you didn't do this the first time around, please write this one in big letters and put it on your fridge.

Major Acting Key.

The life of your acting depends on your ability to be available to and responsive to everything that is actually happening as it is happening.

Let's break it down again into smaller chunks.

The life of your acting depends on your ability to be available to and responsive to everything that is actually happening as it is happening.

1. "The life." You must be the arrow, aiming for the creation of life itself, nothing less. The mission is to bring life itself to the stage and in front of the camera, not the

approximation of life, not the representation of life, not the pretense or semblance of life, but life itself.

2. "Your Ability." You have worked relentlessly to hone your skills, to reinvigorate and revive your innate human facilities and then apply them to your craft as an actor.

3. "Available." You listen with the ear of your heart, sensitized to what is going on in "the others", and in the world around you, at an intuitive level.

4. "Responsive." You get yourself out of the way so that your instinct can function and you can become the full expression of your truthful point of view. You permit "it" to lead.

5. "To Everything." You embrace everything and deny nothing. You have become adept at working with every bit of behavior coming your way from your acting partners and from the world of the play. You do not pause to consider what is worth responding to, you respond to all of it.

6. "Actually Happening." You are aware of, and you are working with, what is actually being given to you rather than what worked during last night's performance, or back in rehearsal, or what you would prefer to be happening.

7. "As it is Happening." You are attentive to every moment. You live right now, right now, right now. You do not get caught in the trap of anticipating what is coming next and you are not stuck in your head going over what you wish would have happened or what you think

should have happened in any moment that has already gone by.

❖❖❖

Continuing with the "doing":

So you have named your doing and you have begun to explore it with your partner.

There is still something missing.

Please consider this:

Just like human beings in life...

What the character is doing comes from a need.

And now you, the actor, must do "the doing" that the character is doing.

Hold on a moment...

There is a problem.

The character has the need to do the doing, but you don't.

Your job now is to make the character's need to do the doing your need to do the doing.

Sound familiar?

Yes, it is the same kind of process I told you about in the chapter on acting component two, meaning. The process we discussed for the deeper wish, as you may remember, is called, "personalizing the point of view of the character."

In personalizing the character's point of view, you were stepping inside the deeper wish of the character, their core desire that then manifests in everything they are fighting for in the play.

Now, you must do the very same thing for each of the doings, you must personalize the doing so that you have the authentic need to do it.

As Harry, in the scene we have been working with for instance, when you are "encouraging" Darlene, you must actually need to do that.

The way to do this is quite simple.

It is a simple question you must ask yourself.

The question includes two very simple words.

The two words are:

"as if."

The question is:

"This is "as if" what is happening for me?"

This question will help guide you towards discovering an analogous circumstance from both your imagination and your life that once rooted in you, will give you the need to do the doing.

And...

I have an exquisite way for you to personalize the doing.

It is powerful and leads to an authentic need to do the doing that will live in your veins so that you no longer have to think about it.

To learn my process I call, "personalize the doing" go to this link:

www.trueactinginstitute.com/learn

I have one more acting element to explore with you here in the book.

I saved it for last.

I have not uttered this word until now.

Why?

The word I am about to give you, when related to acting, has caused more confusion, self-consciousness, pushing and straining, stress, worry, acting paralysis and fear than any other word in the actors vocabulary.

But not just for the actor.

The following is also true:

The word I am about to give you, when related to much of the teaching of acting, has caused more confusion, self-consciousness, pushing and straining, stress, worry, teaching paralysis and fear than any other word in the acting teachers vocabulary.

For the actor...

The worry, self-consciousness and fear begins in the acting classroom and often plagues the actor for the rest of his acting career.

The word is:

Emotion

❖❖❖

The truth is, the issue of emotion related to acting is utterly simple.

I am going to show you.

I want you to breathe freely again.

I want to take away your fear and worry about this thing called emotion and your acting.

Sound good?

❖❖❖

Yet there is a challenge.

Let's define the challenge.

To do this:

Let's begin with life.

As a human organism, you are an emotional being.

Let's call you:

An emotional instrument.

At the time of your birth, you popped out of your Mom playing a whole range of emotional notes.

And...

Your emotions were freely expressed, without effort or thought.

For quite a while, you had no judgement about any particular emotion. There was no "this emotion is a good one" or, "this emotion is a bad one."

You had no concern about what anyone thought about you for expressing any particular emotion.
You had no fear that if you felt something deeply you would go crazy.

You permitted yourself to experience and express the most intense emotions possible and, when the emotion subsided, you were just fine.

You didn't waste a moment criticizing yourself for having emotional responses.

Whether your emotions were huge and powerful or more quiet and internal, you accepted all of them as they flowed through you and then you simply moved on to whatever came next.

Then you grew up.

You were warned to "Pull yourself together."

You were told to "Get your act together."

You got all clogged up.

Your emotions got all clogged up.

Flash forward.

Now...

As an actor...

You must unclog yourself.

As you do...

You will reclaim all of the notes your were meant to play in this life.

You see...

Until you unclog, you will be limited to playing the same song over and over.

We are talking about freedom.

The freedom to be.

When you shed the acquired self, the true self, the self that is yet to be discovered, will be set free. This is when "it" can lead.

I will not tell you how to unclog yourself.

I will only tell you that it must begin with a tremendous desire and unrelenting, single-minded and unbending commitment to do it.

Onward friends...

Emotions and acting.

In life, your emotions are connected to things that are meaningful to you.

When you have a need, it is clear that emotion is an intrinsic part of the need.

The stronger the need, the stronger the emotion.

The need sends you out into the world to do something to fulfill that need.

If your attempt to satisfy your need goes well, the fulfillment of your need will result in one arena of emotional responses, with emotions such as:

Joy, bliss, delight, satisfaction, ecstasy, gladness, jubilance, euphoria, happiness, contentment, elation, exhilaration, content, etc.

If your attempt to satisfy your need does not go well, the failure to fulfill your need will result in a very different arena of emotional responses, with emotions such as:

Despair, anguish, gloom, misery, sorrow, dejection, disheartenment, forlornness, grief, sadness, unhappiness, heartache, melancholy, worry, despondency, etc.

This is all pretty obvious and there is no mystery.

The same is true with acting.

It is obvious and there is no mystery.

Emotion in acting is simply a result of this basic math:

True Need + Meaningful Doing = Real Emotional Responses

Read this again please:

True Need + Meaningful Doing = Real Emotional Responses
You see?

It goes like this:

When you have personalized the deep desire of the character, you now have a true need.

When you have personalized the things you must do as the character, you have meaningful doing.

134

When you put these two powerful forces together they result in:

Real emotional responses.

❖❖❖

Let me expand...

Here's the glorious beauty of it:

When you have personalized the deep desire of the character, you now have a true need.

When you have personalized the things you must do as the character, you have meaningful doing.

When you put these two powerful forces together they result in:

Real emotional responses that are out of your control!

Oh yes, this is big, very big.

I say it again:

When you put these two powerful forces together they result in:

Real emotional responses that are out of your control!

What do I mean by "out of your control?"

What I mean is:

You don't have to think about them!

Wow!

Yes, you do not have to try and be emotional!

Wow!

Imagine that!

An actor who does not have to try to be emotional!

To see an actor working who is not trying to be emotional!

Man, is that ever a breath of fresh air!

So rare, so beautiful, so extraordinary!!

I know, I know, I can't stop adding exclamation points!!

It's going overboard, I know!!!

But I can't help myself!!!!

This so, so huge!!!!!!

This is so completely revolutionary!!!!!!!!!!

Somebody help me!!!!!!!!!!!!!!!!!!!

Get me away from this keyboard!!!!!!!!!!!!!!!!!!!!!!!!!!!!!!!!!!

❖❖❖

Facts of emotion and acting:

In life, we do not pay much attention to how "big" or "little" our emotional responses are and we rarely, if ever, sit around trying to be emotional.

Who does this?

Only actors.

It is:

- Rare to see an actor who is not trying to be emotional.

- Rare to see an actor who is not trying to show us how emotional he is.

- Rare to see an actor who does not have his attention on himself, checking out whether he is emotional enough.

- Rare to see an actor who is not busy congratulating himself for having an emotional moment.

It is:

- No fun to watch an actor trying to be emotional.

- No fun to watch an actor trying to show us how emotional he is.

- No fun to watch an actor with his attention on himself, checking out if he is being emotional enough.

- No fun to watch an actor congratulating himself for having an emotional moment.

Emotion and acting continued...

Imagine you are driving your two year old daughter to day care. She is in her car seat in the back. The road is very busy with rush hour traffic. A car to your left gets so close to you that it touches your door. You panic and swerve your car to the right and into the median where you crash the front of your car into some metal fencing. Your face hits the windshield and you are dizzy.

Imagine that you look back to check on your daughter and as you turn back to the front, you notice the hood of the car is smoking. Suddenly there are flames. You jump out of the car and pull on the back door to get your daughter out of her car seat and out of the car. The door is jammed. You pull at it with great force. You are screaming. The door opens and you work at releasing your daughter from her car seat. The latch on the seat belt holding her in the car seat is stuck so you start to yank at the whole seat to get the car seat and your little girl away from the car.

Pause...

This is an intense and extreme set of imaginary circumstances.

Just reading it might have triggered a powerful emotional response in you.

Please consider these important questions:

1. As you are trying to get your little girl out of her car seat, would you have any thoughts whatsoever about your emotions or if you are being emotional enough?

No, you wouldn't, only actors do.

2. As you are trying to get your little girl out of her car seat, would you stop to break down and cry so that all the people driving by would believe that you are an emotional person?

No, you wouldn't, only actors do.

The point is:

In life, your complete attention would be on one thing only, getting your little girl away from the car. You would certainly have all kinds of powerful emotional responses.

You would have all kinds of powerful emotional responses AND your complete attention and effort would be directed to what you are doing, saving your little girl!

Obvious, yes?

Yes, it is.

This imaginary example makes crystal clear that:

True Need + Meaningful Doing = Real Emotional Responses

To witness an actor who is not trying to be emotional but in every moment is fighting for all he's worth to accomplish the thing which is authentically, personally meaningful to him, the mission which he has made essential, vital and urgent, who is in continual relationship with his partners on stage and with the world around him and who is open and free, spontaneous and emotionally alive, continually in adjustment to every subtle new ounce of behavior coming his way, embracing and responsive to everything that is happening as it is happening, now that is something to write home about.

Give this some thought.

Isn't it interesting that when you go to see a movie, you sit there in the dark and suddenly - without any effort or thought - you find yourself laughing hysterically or sobbing uncontrollably or having all kinds of intense emotional reactions?

It comes so easy and unexpectedly.

How does this happen do you think?

It happens because you are relaxed, you have no predetermined ideas about how you should feel, you have nothing to prove and so you turn yourself over and loosen the controls.

It is a very useful thing to bring this kind of inner relaxation to your acting.

"But!" you say...

"But the other character has a line in the scene where he asks me to please stop crying. I have to cry. Help!"

You're right, you do.

The truth is...

Plays and movies are about huge events in the lives of the characters and in every play and movie that you act in, there will be moments that you will have to fulfill the very strong emotional demands placed on you.

There is a way to do this. It is completely organic and healthy and liberating.

To learn more about working with your "emotional instrument" go to this link:

www.trueactinginstitute.com/learn

One last note about emotions and acting.

Please remember this:

When the audience comes to see you in the play or movie, they have no preconceived ideas about how you should be emotionally, they have no emotional expectations and they do not come to judge your ability to be emotional.

The audience will accept any reaction you have if it is true.

That is the key.

The audience has a deeply seated, inner bullshit meter.

There is true and alive. There is fake and lifeless.

They know the difference.

❖❖❖

Chapter Twelve.

Wrapping Up.

I have a couple of notes for you here and then I will let you go.

1.

Many scientists have recognized that the greatest mystery known to man is human consciousness. One thing we do know is that whatever that thing you call "you" actually is, you have a marvelous creation called a "body" that carries you around.

Earlier in the book, I told you...

"Please note, I am not addressing things like your physical conditioning, flexibility and endurance as well as working on your vocal instrument and your diction which are essential if your aim is to act professionally. How could an actor possibly leave these out? You would be surprised how many do."

I am adding this:

The actor must be an athlete.

The actor must be an athlete of the mind, the heart and the body.

You must not leave out the body.

The actor must be continually awake and alert and "locked in" as basketball players like to say.

The actor must be prepared to bring vast amounts of mental, emotional and physical energy to every project he works on, to every performance of the play, to every take in front of the camera.

You must have a strong, nimble, limber and agile body, (which includes your vocal instrument) to carry you around and to do the work you will be required to do.

Train that body of yours.

❖❖❖

2.

Mastering my three components of true acting - relationship, meaning and movement - naturally raise your acting to what I call the top 5%.

The practice has a huge payoff. Some of the results are listed here:

• You conquer the double bind: being natural on purpose.

• You live "full out" without any effort or tension.

• You are captivating and compelling to the audience without trying to entertain them.

- You achieve utter simplicity.

- You trust that doing no more than necessary is enough.

- You paint with your own unique palette of personal meaning.

- Everything you do is purposeful.

- You consistently ride on the flow of creation.

- You are willing and able to leap into the unknown in each performance rather than relying on what seemed to work before.

- You arrive at complete emotional freedom.

- You become deeply relaxed and vibrantly alert at the very same time.

- You embrace everything and deny nothing.

- You listen with the ear of your heart.

❖❖❖

3.

One last nugget of gold.

Mastery of my three simple components of acting has one more key payoff:

Acting becomes fun for you.

And...

When acting is fun for you, it is fun for the audience too.

It has to be fun.

It has to be fun no matter the set of circumstances the script requires you to live out.

It is the joy of expression.

It is the great joy of being witnessed by the audience who comes to complete the circuit of electricity your performance radiates across the footlights.

Thank you for your attention dear friend,

Larry

❖❖❖

A Secret Bonus.

A list of powerful quotes. A thank you for spending this time with me.

Talk doesn't cook rice.

CHINESE PROVERB

Care about people's approval, and you will be their prisoner.

CHINESE PROVERB

If you let yourself be blown to and fro, you lose touch with your roots.

CHINESE PROVERB

The journey of a thousand miles begins with a single step.

LAO-TSE

Your vision will become clear only when you can look into your own heart.

CARL JUNG

The past has flown away. The coming month and year do not exist. Ours only is the present's tiny point.

MAHMUD SHABISTARI

If a man carries his own lantern, he need not fear darkness.

HASIDIC SAYING

Worry never robs tomorrow of its sorrow; it only saps today of its strength.

A.J. CRONIN

If we do not change our direction, we are likely to end up where we are headed.

ANCIENT CHINESE PROVERB

To improve the golden moment of opportunity, and catch the good that is within our reach, is the great art of life.

SAMUEL JOHNSON

The ability to simplify means to eliminate the unnecessary so that the necessary may speak.

HANS HOFMANN

It is the chiefest point of happiness that a man is willing to be what he is.

DESIDERIUS ERASMUS

We are what we repeatedly do. Excellence, then, is not an act, but a habit.

ARISTOTLE

If one advances confidently in the direction of his dreams, and endeavors to live the life which he has imagined, he will meet with success unexpected in common hours.

HENRY DAVID THOREAU

If you understand, things are just as they are; if you do not understand, things are just as they are.

ZEN PROVERB

The intellect has little to do on the road to discovery. There comes a leap in consciousness, call it intuition or what you will, and the solution comes to you and you don't know how or why.

ALBERT EINSTEIN

All the beautiful sentiments in the world weigh less than a single lovely action.

JAMES RUSSELL LOWELL

Real generosity toward the future consists in giving all to what is present.

ALBERT CAMUS

If you work on your mind with your mind, how can you avoid an immense confusion?

SENG-TS'AN

It does not matter how slowly you go, so long as you do not stop.

CONFUCIUS

If you have built castles in the air, your work need not be lost; that is where they should be. Now put foundations under them.

HENRY DAVID THOREAU

Great Spirit, help me never to judge another until I have walked in his moccasins.

SIOUX INDIAN PRAYER

The harder we try to catch hold of the moment, to seize a pleasant sensation, the more elusive it becomes. It is like trying to clutch water in one's hands—the harder one grips, the faster it slips through one's fingers.

ALAN WATTS

Remind me each day that the race is not always to the swift; that there is more to life than increasing its speed. Let me look upward into the towering oak and know that it grew great and strong because it grew slowly and well.

ORIN L. CRAIN

Your proper concern is alone the action of duty, not the fruits of the action. Cast then away all desire and fear for the fruits, and perform your duty.

BHAGAVAD GITA

Life can only be understood backwards, but it must be lived forwards.

SOREN KIERKEGAARD

Even if I knew that tomorrow the world would go to pieces, I would still plant my apple tree.

MARTIN LUTHER

Art is a collaboration between God and the artist, and the less the artist does the better.

ANDRE GIDE

I saw the angel in the marble and carved until I set him free.

MICHELANGELO

Art attracts us only by what it reveals of our most secret self.

JEAN-LUC GODARD

If you ask me what I came to do in this world, I, an artist, I will answer you: 'I came to live out loud.'

EMILE ZOLA

Growth demands a temporary surrender of security.

GAIL SHEEHY

All growth is a leap in the dark, a spontaneous unpremeditated act without the benefit of experience.

HENRY MILLER

Life is either a daring adventure or nothing. To keep our faces toward change and behave like free spirits in the presence of fate is strength undefeatable.

HELEN KELLER

Make the most of yourself, for that is all there is of you.

RALPH WALDO EMERSON

We should take care not to make the intellect our god; it has, of course, powerful muscles, but no personality.

ALBERT EINSTEIN

A good heart is better than all the heads in the world.

EDWARD BULWER-LYTTON

What lies behind us and what lies before us are tiny matters compared to what lies within us.

OLIVER WENDELL HOLMES

Critics are like eunuchs in a harem: they know how it's done, they've seen it done every day, but they're unable to do it themselves.

BRENDAN BEHAN

A bad review is even less important than whether it is raining in Patagonia.

IRIS MURDOCH

The public is the only critic whose opinion is worth anything at all.

MARK TWAIN

Pay no attention to what the critics say; no statue has ever been erected to a critic.

JEAN SIBELIUS

The expectations of life depend upon diligence; the mechanic that would perfect his work must first sharpen his tools.

CONFUCIUS

Amateurs hope. Professionals work.

GARSON KANIN

It is no use saying, 'We are doing our best.' You have got to succeed in doing what is necessary.

WINSTON CHURCHILL

The only place where success comes before work is in a dictionary.

VIDAL SASSOON

The winds and waves are always on the side of the ablest navigators.

EDWARD GIBBON

I long to accomplish a great and noble task, but it is my chief duty to accomplish small tasks as if they were great and noble.

HELEN KELLER

Nothing is more simple than greatness; indeed, to be simple is to be great.

RALPH WALDO EMERSON

Many persons have a wrong idea of what constitutes true happiness. It is not attained through self-gratification but through fidelity to a worthy purpose.

HELEN KELLER

Winning is important, but what brings me real joy is the experience of being fully engaged in whatever I'm doing.

PHIL JACKSON

Cherish your visions and your dreams as they are the children of your soul; the blue prints of your ultimate achievements.

NAPOLEON HILL

You see things; and you say 'Why?' But I dream things that never were; and I say 'Why not?'

GEORGE BERNARD SHAW

Some of the world's greatest feats were accomplished by people not smart enough to know they were impossible.

DOUG LARSON

Real love is a pilgrimage. It happens when there is no strategy, but it is very rare because most people are strategists.

ANITA BROOKNER

Darkness cannot drive out darkness; only light can do that. Hate cannot drive out hate; only love can do that.

MARTIN LUTHER KING JR.

No love, no friendship can cross the path of our destiny without leaving some mark on it forever.

FRANCOIS MAURIAC

Be glad of life, because it gives you the chance to love and to work and to play and to look up at the stars.

HENRY VAN DYKE

Still around the corner there may wait a new road, or a secret gate.

J.R.R. TOLKIEN

There is not enough darkness in the world to put out the light of even one small candle.

ROBERT ALDEN